9-10

8506

With Maxi and Mini in Muffkinland

By V. Gilbert Beers

Illustrated by Helen Endres

MOODY PRESS • CHICAGO

What You Will Find in This Book

Library of Congress Cataloging in Publication Data

Beers, Victor Gilbert, 1928-
  With Maxi and Mini in Muffkinland.
  (The Muffin Family Picture Bible)
  SUMMARY: Selected Bible stories accompanied by corresponding contemporary stories involving the imaginary Muffin Family.
  1. Bible stories, English. I. Title.
BS551. 2. B4525   220.9' 505   80-39767
ISBN 0-8024-4063-0

Printed in the United States of America

To Parents and Teachers

One of the most important jobs for parent or teacher is to help increase a child's desire for the Word of God. With that desire, the Bible will be read, studied, memorized, applied to life, and shared. Without it, the Bible will become for that person a forgotten Book on a dusty shelf.

But it is not easy today to compete for a child's interest in a world dominated by multi-million-dollar TV ads that come on fast, hit hard, and leave the child staggering with their demands and appeals. Some have felt a sense of hopelessness in trying to compete, especially in presenting the Bible, which is difficult for even an adult to pursue with excitement.

The Muffin Family is not a five-star TV production. We do not want it that way. But it is a simple, interesting presentation of Bible and life, lived out in a family just like yours, with children just like yours. There is reality, so that families say, "That's us!" But there is also fantasy in the Muffin Family adventures that take us *Across Buttonwood Bridge, Through Golden Windows, Under the Tagalong Tree, With Sails to the Wind, From Castles in the Clouds,* and now *With Maxi and Mini in Muffkinland.* There, in these delightful, make-believe places, Bible and life, reality and fantasy, fun and life's most important values meet–an important intersection to shape the whole person for Jesus.

A Time for Miracles

A Small Gift for Five Thousand People

Matthew 14:13-21; Mark 6:30-44; Luke 9:10-17; John 6:1-15

"May I go, too?" a boy panted as he ran into his house.

"Where?" asked his mother. "With whom?"

"With everyone!" the boy answered. "Jesus is going by boat to that lonely hill over there. Everyone is going along the road to meet Him. Please may I go too?"

"Of course," the mother answered. "I wish I could go, too, but I can't. Hurry and wash while I get some food for you to take. You may need it."

The boy grumbled a little about washing, but he did it. By the time he had finished, his mother had put two dried fish and five little loaves of bread into a basket.

The mother smiled as the boy ran through the door with the little basket and headed down the road. She was glad her boy wanted to see and hear Jesus. She had heard Him say many wonderful things about God.

It was early afternoon by the time the boy reached the lonely hill. But it wasn't lonely now. It was filled with people who had come to hear Jesus.

How can I find Him? the boy wondered.

The boy squeezed his way through the crowd. He had never seen so many people in one place before. At last he found a place near the front where he could see and hear Jesus.

6

Jesus talked about many things. He told about God and how people might know Him. He told about heaven and how people might go there.

The boy noticed how quiet the large crowd was. The people listened carefully to every word that Jesus said. Many people came to Jesus, and He healed them.

But toward evening, some of Jesus' friends talked with Him. The boy could hear what they said.

"There is no food here in this lonely place," they told Jesus. "Should we send the people into the towns to buy food?"

The boy was surprised to hear what Jesus said. "No, you give them something to eat," He told His friends.

"But where shall we get the food for so many people?" they asked. "Shall we go into the towns to buy bread for all these people?"

"Find out first how much food we have here," Jesus answered.

Jesus' friends walked through the crowd. "Does anyone have any food?" they called to the people.

The boy could hardly believe it. Not one person in that crowd had thought to bring food except him.

"I have five small loaves of bread and two fish," the boy said. "It isn't much, but Jesus may have it."

Jesus' friends told Him about the boy's food. "But how can we feed thousands of people with so little?" they asked Him.

Jesus told them to seat the people on the grass in groups of hundreds and fifties. When they were seated, everyone became quiet as Jesus prayed, thanking God for the food.

Then Jesus began to break the boy's bread and fish into pieces. His friends carried the pieces in baskets to the people. Back and forth they went, again and again.

The boy could hardly believe it! Jesus was still breaking pieces from his loaves and fish. How did He do it? How could his small gift feed so many?

At last everyone had as much as he wanted to eat. Jesus' friends picked up what was left over. There were twelve baskets full of scraps.

Later, as the crowd began to leave, the boy sat quietly watching Jesus. Again and again he wondered, *Who is this Man, and how could He feed five thousand people with my five small loaves and two fish?* Some day he would ask Him, but now he must go home.

WHAT DO YOU THINK?
What this story teaches: Jesus can do wonderful things with our small gifts.
1. What kind of gift did the boy have to offer Jesus? What did Jesus do with that small gift?
2. Does Jesus expect big, expensive gifts, or will He gladly accept small gifts, too? Can He do big things with small gifts, or must He have big gifts in order to do big things?

Two Small Gifts

Once there were two Muffkins who lived in Muffkinland. Givvy Muffkin was wise and loyal to his king. Greedy Muffkin was selfish and not so loyal. But both were quite hungry, for food had become scarce among the Muffkins.

One day the two Muffkins set out to seek their fortune, which they hoped would be something to eat. They looked near and far until at last they came to a hidden treasure, ten grains of corn.

Greedy Muffkin rubbed his hands in glee. "We will divide the grains of corn," he said. "Four for you and six for me!"

Givvy Muffkin watched Greedy Muffkin scoop up six grains, which were really quite much for a Muffkin to handle, pop them into a big sack, and head toward home. Then Givvy carefully placed his four grains into his sack and headed home, too, whistling as he went.

As one would expect, Greedy Muffkin hurried into his Muffkin hole with his bag and put the six grains of corn in his pantry. He would feast on them alone for many weeks to come. No one else would share his treasure!

Givvy thought once about going straight home to put his four grains in his pantry. But when he saw the palace, he remembered the king and wanted to share his good fortune with him.

Without another thought, Givvy headed toward the palace to see the king. He laid his bag of treasure before the king and told about his wonderful find.

"I want to share my fortune with my king," Givvy told him. "Two grains for you and two grains for me."

The king smiled. Two grains of corn for a king may not seem like much, but they were half of Givvy's treasure.

"I thank you with all my heart," said the king. "Your two grains will become a royal feast for all the kingdom."

"But how can that be?" asked Givvy.

"By five miracles," the king answered.

The king took the two grains of corn into his hands and tucked them under the soft warm soil in the palace garden. "The miracle of the soil is God's first miracle," the king told Givvy.

A big cloud moved across the sun and dropped its rain upon the soil. Soon the thirsty soil and the grains of corn were watered. "The miracle of the rain is God's second miracle," said the king.

The cloud moved away, and the sun smiled upon the palace garden. The moist soil grew warm, like a cozy blanket over the grains of corn. "That is God's third miracle," the king told Givvy. "The rain and soil need His warm sunshine to make our royal feast."

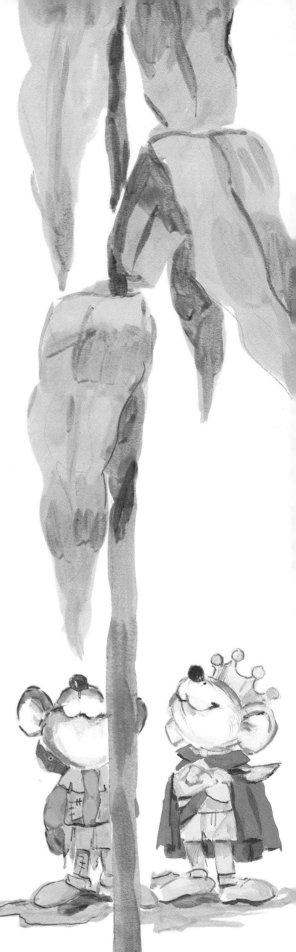

One day Givvy and the king saw two beautiful green shoots peeking through the soil in the palace garden. They grew quickly until they were strong green stalks of corn, taller than the palace itself. "God's fourth miracle is new life," said the king. "Your two grains of corn have died, and from them have come forth these beautiful new stalks."

Each day Givvy and the king watched as two ears of corn grew on them, becoming larger and larger. By autumn, when the leaves fell and the first cold winds swept down from the north, the stalks turned golden brown and rustled in the winds. The king ordered his workmen to climb into the tall stalks and cut down the golden ears of corn.

There was much excitement in Muffkinland as the great ears of corn fell to the ground. Trumpets sounded and the king's decree was read, inviting all the Muffkins to the royal banquet.

"You have now seen the fifth miracle," the king told Givvy. "It is God's miracle of multiplication. From your two seeds He has made two hundred and more. And now your two seeds have become a royal feast for all our people."

And what a royal feast that was as the Muffkins gathered in the king's banquet hall! Of course, you can imagine that Givvy was the guest of honor, for they feasted on his two small gifts, touched by God's five miracles.

LET'S TALK ABOUT THIS
What this story teaches: We should give even our smallest gifts to Jesus, for mighty miracles may come from them.

1. What kind of Muffkin was Greedy? Where do you think Greedy was during the royal feast? What kind of Muffkin was Givvy? How do you know?
2. How did Givvy's small gifts become a royal feast? Can you name God's five miracles in this story? Will you thank Him for each one?

11

Walking on the Water

Matthew 14: 22-33; Mark 6: 45-52; John 6: 16-21

By the time Jesus' disciples had picked up the last scraps of bread and fish, the sun was setting. More than five thousand people had been fed with only five loaves and two fish. The people still lingered, waiting to see if Jesus would do some other wonderful miracle for them.

But there would be no other miracle for the crowd tonight. It was time to go home. Jesus urged His disciples to leave by boat for Bethsaida. He would follow later.

As the disciples rowed from shore, they saw that Jesus was sending the crowd away. When the last person was gone, Jesus walked alone to the top of the mountain where He had fed the people, and began to pray.

The disciples lifted the sails on their fishing boat and headed into the wind. But they had not gone far before the wind picked up, blowing across the sea until the waves pounded against their boat.

"The wind is too strong!" someone shouted. "We'll have to row!" The disciples grabbed the oars again and rowed frantically against the wind and the waves.

The last light of evening faded from the sky, and the night stars appeared. But the wind kept howling around the small fishing boat.

Throughout the night, the disciples kept on rowing. By early morning, two or three hours before sunrise, their backs ached and their hands were sore.

"What will we do?" one of the disciples shouted above the noise of the wind.

"I say we should quit and drift with the wind," another grumbled. "We're only halfway home! We'll never make it!"

Suddenly a third disciple stopped rowing and pointed toward the raging sea. "Look!" he cried out. "A ghost!"

Everyone stopped rowing now and looked out into the darkness. A light figure was coming toward them across the sea.

"Row!" shouted some of the disciples. "Hurry!"

All of the men grabbed their oars and rowed with all their might. But the light figure came closer and closer. At last it was even with the boat.

"You must not be afraid." A voice spoke from the ghostly figure.

"That's Jesus' voice!" one of the men said. "He's walking on those stormy waves as though they were dry land!"

"It is I," said Jesus. "You must not be afraid."

Peter was excited now when he saw that it was Jesus walking on the water. "Lord, command me to come across the water to you," he shouted.

"Come!" Jesus commanded.

Peter climbed from the boat while all the other disciples stared at him. Their mouths fell open as they saw Peter walk across the water toward Jesus.

But Peter had found it easier in the boat than on the water. He suddenly realized what he was doing, and he became afraid. Then he began to sink.

"Help me, Lord!" he cried out to Jesus.

Jesus reached out His hand and lifted Peter up. "Why did you doubt?" Jesus asked. "You have such little faith."

Before long, Jesus and Peter stepped into the fishing boat. As soon as they did, the wind stopped and the sea became calm.

The disciples stared at Jesus. He had not only walked across the stormy water, but He had caused the wind to stop and the sea to grow calm.

"You certainly are God's Son!" they said. "No one else could do such marvelous things!"

WHAT DO YOU THINK?

What this story teaches: Jesus is certainly God's Son, for no one else could do the marvelous things that He did.

1. Who is Jesus? What did you learn from this story?

2. How do you know that Jesus is God's Son? Can anyone else do what He did?

3. Would you want to accept an ordinary man as your Savior? Would you want to accept Jesus, God's Son, as your Savior?

A Million Times More than a Poppi

"Isn't it a BE-YOOtiful evening to go canoeing?" Mini crooned.

Maxi grunted a little as he shoved the canoe away from the beach at Lake Pleasant. He was glad Mommi and Poppi were watching, for he could show them how well he could do the J stroke now.

Maxi and Mini slipped their paddles into the water and headed away from the campground. It really was a beautiful evening. Only a few clouds were in the sky above the lake.

Mommi had not been quite so sure that it was safe for Maxi and Mini to go alone in the canoe, but Poppi had reminded her that both of them were good swimmers. Anyway, there was a firm rule in the Muffin Family to remain with a boat if it should tip over. So, when Maxi and Mini agreed to wear life vests and "be careful," Mommi and Poppi let them go.

"Be back before dark!" Maxi heard Poppi call from the campground. Maxi waved to show that he heard Poppi and then showed off with what he thought was a perfect J stroke.

Maxi and Mini chattered about the beautiful hills and tall trees surrounding the lake and the fun they were having camping together as a family. They talked about the campfire the night before, the stars, and a dozen or more other things.

Suddenly Maxi realized that the waves on the lake were much higher. A strong wind had come up behind them, blowing them farther than they had wanted to go from the campground.

"We've got to head back," Maxi urged. "The sun is setting, and we promised to be back by dark."

But when Maxi and Mini turned the canoe around, they found that the easy canoeing they had been having with the wind was not going to be so easy now. In fact, it was going to be very hard!

15

The waves were getting so high now that they splashed across the front of the canoe, sending water onto Maxi and Mini. It was suddenly quite clear that they had gone much too far and that the wind was blowing much too hard for them.

"Pull hard!" Maxi called to Mini.

"I'm trying!" Mini complained.

Maxi and Mini paddled as hard as they could. But it seemed that they were not going very far. By now the sun was down, and the wind was getting cooler.

Maxi grunted as he tried to put more muscle into each stroke. Before long, Mini began to cry.

"I'm tired, Maxi!" she sobbed. "I can't make another stroke!"

"I'm tired, too," Maxi answered. "But if we don't keep rowing, we'll be blown back into the middle of the lake."

Just then a voice called out. "Ahoy there, mates! Want to catch a bus home?"

It was Poppi! Maxi and Mini had been so busy paddling that they had not seen him come out in the rowboat.

Poppi pulled alongside the canoe and helped Maxi and Mini into the rowboat with him. Then he tied the canoe's anchor rope to the rowboat and headed toward the campground.

Maxi watched as Poppi made long powerful strokes with the oars. Suddenly he realized how much stronger Poppi was. He was taking two boats and three of them home at a much faster speed than Maxi and Mini went with just the canoe.

"Poppi, how much more can you do than I can do?" Maxi asked.

"Five times? Ten times?" Poppi answered. "Who knows? But think how much more Jesus can do than I can do. A million times? A billion times?"

Maxi began to think about that. If Poppi could do five times more than Maxi, and Jesus could do a million times more than Poppi, Jesus must really be Someone special.

That night, around the campfire, Poppi told Maxi and Mini the story about Jesus' walking on the water. He told how Jesus had caused the wind and waves to die down.

"The way I helped you this evening is Poppi stuff," he said. "Most other poppis could do that, too. But no poppi in the world could do what Jesus did. That's because Jesus is God's Son."

"I'm glad Jesus is our friend," said Mini. "I wouldn't want Him to zap me."

"I'm glad He's our friend, too," said Poppi. "But now it's off to bed with you two, or Mommi and I will zap you."

Before long, Maxi and Mini were sound asleep, dreaming about the wind and waves on Lake Pleasant...or was it the Sea of Galilee?

LET'S TALK ABOUT THIS

What this story teaches: Children often need poppis and mommis to help them, for mommis and poppis can do much more than children can; but everyone needs Jesus, God's Son, for He can do much, much more than any of us.

1. How much more can a poppi do than a Maxi or Mini? Ten times? A hundred times? How much more can Jesus do than a poppi or mommi? A million times? A billion times?

2. Are you glad Jesus is your friend? Have you asked Him to be with you each day as your friend and Savior?

Good News

Matthew 14: 34-36; Mark 6: 53-56

One bright and sunny day Jesus and His disciples left their village by boat and sailed westward across the Sea of Galilee. Along the way they must have talked about the windy night when they had rowed across the sea. They must have laughed and teased each other about the "ghost" they had seen when Jesus walked upon the water to meet them.

Everyone was happy as they landed on the shore of a large, rich valley called Gennesaret, on the northwestern side of the sea. It was filled with olive trees, vineyards, palms, melons, and vegetables.

As soon as Jesus landed, people began to crowd around him. Many ran off to find their friends and neighbors, especially those who were sick and needed help.

"Hurry!" they said. "Jesus is here. Bring your sick friends, and He may heal them."

Before long, the narrow roads that led to Gennesaret were filled with people. Some hobbled on crutches. Others were carried on their cots. Still others, who were blind, were led along the way by friends. The deaf, the crippled, those who could not speak, and even those with dreaded leprosy crowded upon the roads. Doctors at that time could not heal them. But they had heard that Jesus could. So they hurried to find Him.

From far and near the people came. Wherever Jesus went, they followed after Him, begging Him to help them and to heal them. When Jesus was in the villages, they swarmed into the marketplaces to find Him. When He was in the countryside, they crowded around Him there.

Many reached out to touch the fringe of His cloak, for they had learned that they might be healed if they could only touch His clothing. Then, when a blind man saw, or a lame man walked again, or a man could speak for the first time, he ran about shouting for joy.

Throughout the Valley of Gennesaret Jesus went, healing and helping those He met. Not one needy person was sent away without His help. It was a day of good news for the people of Gennesaret.

WHAT DO YOU THINK?
What this story teaches: When Jesus heals or helps us, it is a day of good news.
1. What did you learn about Jesus in this story?
2. What kind of people did He help? Did He help only the rich and famous, or did He help anyone and everyone?
3. How do you think the people at Gennesaret felt when Jesus healed them or a friend? How would you have felt?

Bad News, Good News

Deep in the great forest of Muffkinland there lived a poor woodsman with his wife and beautiful young daughter. Some said she was the most beautiful girl Muffkin in all Muffkinland.

The woodsman was a generous man, always helping his friends and neighbors. Naturally, they loved him and his family and often came to visit.

But one day the friends and neighbors whispered something to one another. "Bad news! Bad news!" they said. "The woodsman's beautiful daughter is sick."

The friends and neighbors went to see the woodsman and his wife and daughter. They had many questions to ask.

"Is she very, very sick?"

"How did it happen?"

"What will you do?"

"What can help her get well?"

The poor woodsman sighed. "The king's touch can help her get well," he said.

"Good news! Good news!" said the friends and neighbors.

"But, alas," said the woodsman. "The king is far away in his royal castle. And he is very busy receiving royal guests from faraway lands and taking care of the kingdom. How can I expect the great king to visit my humble cottage?"

"Bad news! Bad news!" the friends and neighbors sighed.

One friend and neighbor went for a long walk to think about the bad news and good news. Givvy Muffkin was sure that the king would help the poor woodsman.

He is a great king who wants to help each person in his kingdom, Givvy thought. *That is good news. But his castle is far away, and it would take days for someone to go there and bring him back. That is bad news.*

Givvy sat down on a big stump by the side of the road to think. Before long, a man came along the road.

"Good afternoon," said Givvy, "and who are you?"

"I am the king's herald," said the man. "I am checking this road so it will be ready for the king as he passes by tomorrow."

"The king will pass by here tomorrow?" Givvy asked with excitement. "That is good news."

"Yes, but he will be very busy, for there is much royal business for him to do," said the herald.

Hm, that is bad news, thought Givvy. But he asked the herald the time when the king would

pass by and ran back to the woodsman's cottage in the forest to tell the news.

"Good news! Good news!" said Givvy. "The king will pass by on the road at the edge of the forest tomorrow."

"Good news! Good news!" the other friends and neighbors said. "We will carry our friend's daughter there to wait for him."

"Ah, but there is also bad news," said Givvy. "The king will be rushing by, for he has much royal business to care for tomorrow."

"Bad news! Bad news!" said the friends and neighbors. "But we will take her there anyway. Perhaps the king will have mercy and stop for a moment so that she may receive the king's touch and get well."

The next day there was much excitement in the deep forest. The woodsman and his friends and neighbors placed the beautiful daughter upon a cot and carried her through the woods to the edge of the road. There they waited until at last they saw the king's royal caravan coming.

"Good news! Good news! The king is coming!" they shouted.

But the king's herald came first. "Stand aside! Stand aside!" he called out. "The king must go through!"

"Bad news! Bad news!" the friends and neighbors said. "We must see the king."

While the friends and neighbors argued with the herald, Givvy slipped quietly away and went to see the king. He bowed low and told the king about the woodsman's daughter.

"Of course, I will help her," said the king. Then he got down from his royal horse and went quietly behind the crowd with Givvy.

"Good news!" Givvy told the woodsman. "The king has come."

The king smiled as he bent down and touched the woodsman's daughter. "Because you have believed in the king's touch, she shall be well!" he said.

As soon as he said that, the beautiful daughter stood up and hugged the woodsman and his wife. She also hugged the king and Givvy!

"Good news! Good news!" the woodsman shouted.

"Good news! Good news!" Givvy shouted, too.

All the other friends and neighbors turned to see what had happened. They then joined in the excitement as they, too, shouted, "Good news!"

"But where is the king?" some asked.

Then they saw him, already riding far down the road, off to finish his royal business.

LET'S TALK ABOUT THIS
What this story teaches: Healing and helping are always good news.

1. How did this story remind you of Jesus' visit to Gennesaret? How did the good news of this story remind you of the good news in that story?

2. Was the Muffkin king interested only in rich and famous people, or did he want to help others, too? How was he like Jesus?

Into the Promised Land

Two Spies and a Scarlet Rope

Joshua 2

"Moses is dead. Joshua will lead us."

For forty years Moses had led the people of Israel through the wilderness. Now Moses was dead. Joshua was the new leader. God had chosen him to be a warrior to lead His people into the land He had promised them.

The Israelites were camped on the eastern side of the Jordan River. The promised land was across the river. Jericho was the first city that must be conquered.

"Go into the land," Joshua told two spies. "See what you can learn about Jericho."

The two Israelite spies crossed the river secretly and made their way to Jericho. They tried to move about the city without raising suspicion, but soon they were discovered.

As night came, the two spies went to the home of a woman named Rahab. "May we have a room for the night?" they asked.

"Yes, but hurry and come in," Rahab answered. "I think you may have been followed."

The men had been followed. Soon word reached the king of Jericho that they had gone to Rahab's house. The king sent soldiers to capture them.

"Bring out those two men who came to your house," the soldiers said. "They are spies who have come to search the land."

But Rahab had already hidden the two spies under some flax that was drying on the flat roof of her house. She knew that the soldiers would not find them there.

"There were two men here," said Rahab. "But they went through the gate about dark. I don't know where they went, but if you hurry, you may still catch them."

The soldiers left quickly and went after the spies. They ordered the gates of the city shut so the spies could not escape if they had stayed behind. Then the soldiers went all the way to the Jordan River, looking for them. But of course they could not find the spies, for they were still on Rahab's roof.

Later that night Rahab came to have a talk with the spies. "I know that the Lord will give you this land," she said. "I know also that your Lord is the true God, for He has helped you in so many ways. When you take this land, please spare me and my family."

"If you help us escape, we will spare you and your family," the spies promised.

Rahab quickly made plans to help them escape. She would find that easy, for her house was built on the wall of the city, with one window toward the outside.

"Climb down this scarlet rope tonight," Rahab told the spies. "Then hide in the mountains for three days until the soldiers stop looking for you."

"Good," said the spies. "But you must keep this scarlet rope tied to your window. When we capture the city, all our soldiers will know they must not harm the people in the house with the scarlet rope. But if the rope is gone, they will not know which house is yours, and you will be killed."

That night the spies slipped quietly down the scarlet rope. Then they hid for three days in the mountains and returned to their camp at last.

Rahab kept her scarlet rope in the window. Not for one minute would she take it away. She knew that it was the only thing that would save her and her family.

WHAT DO YOU THINK?
What this story teaches: It is wise to keep close to that which will save us.
1. What did Rahab do for the spies? What did the spies promise Rahab?
2. Why was the scarlet rope so important to the spies? What did it do for them? Why was it so important to Rahab? What would it do for her? Why was she so careful to keep it in her window at all times?

Car Trouble

By the time the Muffin Family had everything packed and the canoe fastened to the top of the car, the sun was going down. Time had gone so fast at Lake Pleasant, and packing had taken so much longer than Poppi and Mommi had expected, that they were leaving long after they had planned.

"What time will we get home?" Mini asked.

"After midnight, I'm afraid," said Poppi. "But you and Maxi can sleep in the back seat while Mommi and I take turns driving."

As usual, everyone turned for one last look as they pulled away from Lake Pleasant. "Good-bye, good-bye," they called back to the lake. "We love you. Stay beautiful for us, and we'll come back again."

Then everyone laughed about the way this would sound to a stranger in the car. "Family stuff," Mommi said with a smile. "Outsiders almost never understand things like that. But then we don't understand their little family fun things either."

For the first hour or so nobody was sleepy. Mini chattered endlessly about the fun at the lake and the night Poppi came to rescue them from the wind and waves. Maxi tried to get a word in now and then, but it wasn't easy.

At last Mini yawned two or three times, curled up in one corner of the back seat, and was fast asleep. Maxi took up the talking for a while longer, then with a long yawn, he curled up in the other corner and was soon asleep.

Poppi and Mommi talked softly with each other as poppis and mommis do when they don't want to wake their sleeping children. But suddenly in the middle of something Poppi said, the car coughed and sputtered. Then it seemed all right for a few minutes before it coughed and sputtered again.

After this happened two or three times, Poppi pulled into a small rest area beside the highway to look under the hood. As soon as he stopped, the engine died.

"It's beyond me," Poppi told Mommi after he looked under the hood for a while. "I guess I'll never make a good mechanic. Let's see if it starts again."

Poppi tried again and again, but the car would not start. "Now what?" Mommi asked. "It's ten o'clock at night, and we're miles from nowhere."

By this time Maxi and Mini were awake. They also began to ask what they would do. Mini thought they should all walk to the nearest telephone, and Maxi even volunteered to go alone.

"On a lonely highway at ten o'clock at night?" Mommi asked. "I would never let you do that. We won't let Poppi do that either."

"What else can we do?" asked Maxi.

Poppi thought for a moment. "We'll tie a white handkerchief to the door handle and keep the hood raised," he said. "Those are two signals that we need help. Then we'll just wait until someone comes along to help us."

During the next half hour Maxi suggested two or three times that they should "go for it" and walk for a telephone or for help. Then Poppi remembered the Bible story about Rahab and the two spies.

"Even though Jericho was being destroyed, Rahab's home in the city was the safest place she could be," Poppi said. She was safe only when she stayed near it. If she ran into the streets, or tried to escape down the wall, she would surely have been executed."

"What does that have to do with us?" Maxi asked.

"The scarlet rope was her signal for safety," said Poppi. "The white handkerchief and the raised hood are ours. We must always stay near those things that save us."

"That's why we must always stay near Jesus," Mommi added. "He is the only Person who can keep us safe forever, so we need to stay near Him whether we're in trouble or not. So wouldn't it be good to ask Him to help us now?"

The other Muffins thought it would be very good. And they prayed together in the car while they waited for the help they knew would come.

About one-half hour later, a big semitrailer pulled into the rest area. "Need help?" the driver asked with a smile.

When Poppi explained what had happened, the driver looked under the hood. "Here's your problem," he said within a few moments. "Turn the key and let's see what happens."

Poppi smiled as the car purred like a kitten. After he thanked the driver at least four times, he started off, with the semitrailer behind to make sure all was well.

"I never thought of a semitrailer and its driver as a scarlet rope in my window either," Poppi said as he watched the lights in the rearview mirror. "But I'm glad he's staying with us until we're sure things are all right."

But no one answered, for Maxi, Mini, and Mommi were all asleep now.

LET'S TALK ABOUT THIS

What this story teaches: Many things in life can save us from trouble, and we should be grateful for them, just as we should be grateful that Jesus can save us from eternal trouble.

1. How was the semitrailer and its driver like the scarlet rope in Rahab's window? How was the white handkerchief on the car door and the raised hood like Rahab's scarlet rope?

2. Do you like to keep close to those things that protect or save you from trouble? When you realize that Jesus can save you forever, will you want to keep close to Him?

Crossing the Jordan River

Joshua 3-4

"The people of Jericho are afraid of us," the spies reported to Joshua when they returned to camp. "They know that the Lord is helping us."

Joshua smiled. He knew that the Lord was helping them, too. It was time now to enter the promised land, which the Lord had given to His people. Joshua knew that the people needed the Lord's help to cross the Jordan River. Then they needed Him to help conquer their enemies.

"Tomorrow morning we move!" Joshua commanded.

Early the next morning the people packed their tents and all that they had and moved west to the banks of the Jordan River. For three days they waited there for the Lord to tell them what to do.

"How will we get across the river?" people asked.

"Especially now that it is flooded over its banks," said others.

On the third day Joshua sent his officers through the camp of Israel. "Follow the priests who carry God's Ark," they told the people.

Joshua had another important message for the people. "Tomorrow is an important day, for the Lord will do some wonderful things for you," he said. "Tonight you must pray and ask the Lord to forgive your sins and make your life clean and pure, as He wants you to be."

Throughout the camp of Israel that night the people gathered around their campfires to pray. It was a time for forgiveness, a time to become clean and pure. It was also a time when the people pleaded with the Lord to help them cross the Jordan River and settle in their new homeland.

When morning came the people gathered around Joshua to hear what the Lord had said to him. "When you see the wonderful things the Lord will do for you today, you will know that He is with us," Joshua told the people. "You will know also that He will help us conquer our enemies."

The people listened carefully. They knew that the Lord had spoken personally to Joshua.

"The Lord Himself will lead you across the river," Joshua told the people. "Watch the priests who carry the Ark of the Lord. When their feet touch the river, the water upstream will stop flowing and pile up as though an invisible dam were there."

Then Joshua gave orders for the priests to pick up the Ark and walk into the river with it. As their feet touched the water, the river stopped flowing from the north. But the water nearby flowed on to

the south, leaving dry land for the people to walk across.

The priests waited in the middle of the riverbed with the Ark while the people walked across. And what a sight that was, as thousands of Israelites moved across the dry river! Some carried bundles; others drove their wagons and cattle before them.

The hours passed by as a million or more Israelites walked from the east side of the dried-up river into the promised land. For forty years those people and their parents had wandered through the wilderness. They had waited for the day when they could enter the land the Lord had promised them. Now they were entering that land!

Joshua told twelve men, one from each of the twelve tribes, to gather twelve stones from the middle of the river where the priests were standing. "We will build a monument with these stones," Joshua told them. "It will remind us and our children of the wonderful thing that the Lord has done here today."

When the stones had been gathered on shore, and the last Israelite had stepped from the dried-up river, the priests carried the Ark up to where the people stood. As soon as the last priest stepped from the river, the people heard a great roaring noise. Everyone began to shout with excitement as a mighty wall of water rushed down the riverbed, sweeping everything in its path.

That night the people of Israel set up camp at a place called Gilgal. It would be their first night in the promised land, the land the Lord had given them. Forty years of wandering were over.

As the people watched quietly, the twelve stones were laid up into a monument. "When your children ask why these stones are here, tell them about the wonderful things that God did for you today," Joshua told the people. "Let these stones remind you and your families that the Lord is a mighty God, and that you should worship Him forever."

WHAT DO YOU THINK?
What this story teaches: It is good to remind ourselves, and each other, of the wonderful things the Lord has done for us.
1. What was the wonderful thing that the Lord did for the people of Israel at the Jordan River?
2. What did they do to remember this wonderful work that He did for them?

Reminders

"Wow!" Mini whispered when Poppi finished reading about the Israelites crossing the Jordan River. "That would have been scary to go through that river with the water held in place."

"Just like the time the people of Israel crossed the Red Sea," Maxi added. "Except this was a river."

"And that big monument," said Mini. "I wish I could have watched the men make it."

"Why don't we make monuments like that?" Maxi asked.

"Why?" asked Poppi. "What would you do with them?"

Maxi thought for a moment. "Well, the people of Israel used theirs to remind them and their children of the wonderful things God did for them."

Mommi smiled. "Perhaps we do have monuments like that," she said. "But they may look different.

In fact, we may even have some in our house."

Mini's eyes opened wide. "I don't remember any big piles of stones in our house," she said. "Where do you keep them?"

Mommi laughed. "Our monuments aren't big piles of stones," she said. "But if we have a contest for Maxi and Mini, we may find several things that remind us of the wonderful things God has done. Why don't we go through our house to see how many each of you can find? The person with the most wins."

The Muffins started in the kitchen. "There's one!" Maxi shouted. "It's a missionary calendar. It reminds us of God's work among the missionaries."

"Good!" said Poppi.

"Any others?" Mommi asked.

"I see a box of Bible memory cards," Mini said. "Are they like a monument?"

"Yes, they are," said Mommi. "They remind us of the good things God has done for us."

Maxi found some pictures of people, fastened to the refrigerator door with little magnets. "How about these?" he asked. "Aren't these prayer reminders?"

"They are!" said Poppi. "They are missionaries, our pastor, our church, and some friends. Since we open this door often during the day, these pictures remind us to ask God to keep on doing good things for these people, just as He has in the past."

"I have one in my room," said Mini. When the other Muffins followed her, Mini showed them the motto on her wall that said JESUS IS MY BEST FRIEND.

"That certainly tells about some wonderful things God has done through Jesus," said Mommi. "Very good, Mini. That's two for you and two for Maxi."

"I have a Haggai Jar in my room," said Maxi.

"That's no fair," Mini argued. "That's for giving, and it doesn't show what wonderful things God does for us."

"It does, too," Maxi argued back. "It reminds me of the wonderful things God does with our money."

Mini thought for a moment. "OK, you win," she said. So the Muffins went to Maxi's room to look at the Haggai Jar.

In the dining room Mini found a devotional book that Mommi and Poppi read from. "That reminds us of the wonderful things God does," she said, almost expecting Maxi to argue with her. But he didn't.

Mini also pointed to the stereo and said it helped the Muffins remember the good things God does as they listened to records and tapes and the Christian radio station. Then Maxi pointed to the tapes and records of Christian music.

Maxi also pointed to the hymnal on the piano, and Mini said if he could use the hymnal, she could point to the piano itself, for it helped them remember God's wonderful things when Mommi played it.

By the time Maxi and Mini had gone through the entire house with Mommi and Poppi, they had each found seven things that helped the Muffins remember the wonderful things God had done for them.

"Wow! These are better than stone monuments," said Mini.

"And they don't take up nearly as much space," Maxi added with a grin.

"But they do remind us that God does wonderful things," said Mommi.

"And that we should thank Him for them," Poppi added. "So why don't we thank Him right now for His wonderful gifts to us?"

LET'S TALK ABOUT THIS

What this story teaches: There are many small things around us that remind us of the great and wonderful things that God does for us. When we are reminded, we should stop to thank Him for each gift.

1. What are some of the reminders that Mini and Maxi found in their house? What reminders can you find in your house?

2. Can you name ten wonderful things God has done for you and your family? Have you thanked Him for them? Would you like to now?

Saul-The New Man

The New Saul

Acts 9: 1-22

"Why does everyone hate Saul so much?" a boy asked his mother. "Isn't he a Pharisee, a man who works for God?"

"Saul!" his mother answered sharply. "Yes, he is a Pharisee. But he does not work for God."

The boy looked puzzled.

"Saul dresses like a Pharisee," the mother continued. "He goes to the council of religious leaders. He prays and he reads the Scriptures. Then he murders the believers. Is that working for God?"

The boy shook his head to say no.

"Saul would kill us if he came here to Damascus," the mother said. "We had to leave our home and friends in Jerusalem to live in this strange city. Some say Saul may try to come here to kill us and our friends who follow Jesus."

The mother was right. At that very time, Saul was talking with the high priest in Jerusalem, asking for letters that he could take to the synagogues of Damascus. The letters would give Saul permission to capture any of Jesus' followers and take them back to Jerusalem. There he would torture or kill them. He wanted others who followed Jesus to be afraid so they would turn away from Him.

Saul had been torturing Jesus' followers in Jerusalem for some time. It didn't matter to him if the followers were men, women, boys, or girls. If they followed Jesus, they would be hurt, put into prison, or killed.

Now he wanted to carry out his evil work in other cities. He would start in Damascus.

With his letters from the high priest in hand, Saul gathered a band of men who would work with him. Together they headed for Damascus. It was almost one hundred fifty miles away, so the men probably rode on horses.

After a few days, Saul and his helpers approached Damascus. Saul was planning how he might capture Jesus' followers. "How dare they believe in that man Jesus?" he mumbled. "The man is dead, so how can they believe that He is God's Son?"

At that very moment a bright light flashed from the sky. It was much brighter than the sunlight. Saul was so terrified that he fell to the ground.

Suddenly a voice spoke. It seemed to come through the bright light. Saul knew that it was a voice from heaven.

"Saul! Saul!" the voice called out. "Why are you hurting Me?"

Saul trembled when he heard that. "Who...who are you, Lord?" he asked.

"I am Jesus," the voice answered. "You are hurting Me by hurting My people. Now get up and go into Damascus. Someone there will tell you what to do next."

By this time the men with Saul were trembling too. They heard the voice from heaven. But who was speaking?

Saul stumbled to his feet. Now he realized that the bright light had blinded him. His companions took him by the hand and led him into Damascus. There he stayed for three days without eating or drinking.

At the end of the three days, the Lord spoke to a man named Ananias, who also lived in Damascus. "Ananias!" the Lord told him. "Go to the house of a man named Judas, who lives on Straight Street. Ask for Saul, for he is praying."

Ananias was frightened. "But Lord," he argued. "I am one of Your followers, and Saul has been killing and hurting our people. He has come here to Damascus to put our people in chains."

"Go," the Lord ordered. "I have chosen Saul to do My work for Me."

Ananias obeyed without further argument. When he found Saul, he put his hands on Saul's shoulders.

"Brother Saul, the Lord Jesus, Who spoke to you on the way to Damascus, has sent me to you. Be filled with the Holy Spirit and see once more!"

As soon as Ananias said that, Saul could see clearly again. Then he accepted food and ate it.

For several days, Saul remained in Damascus with Jesus' followers. He was no longer Saul, the Pharisee who hurt and murdered Jesus' followers. Now he was Saul, a follower of Jesus. He was a new man. He would never be the same again.

WHAT DO YOU THINK?
What this story teaches: Jesus can change someone in wonderful ways, making that someone a new person.
1. What kind of a person was Saul before Jesus spoke to him? What happened when Jesus spoke to him?
2. What kind of a person do you think Saul was after he became a follower of Jesus?

The New Kid

"What will we do about that new kid down the street?" Maxi asked.

The new kid WAS a problem, so Maxi and Mini had called all their friends in The Problem Solver's Club together to talk about him. Pookie and Charlie were there, and so were Tony and Maria, as well as BoBo.

Pookie was first with a solution. "I say let's gang up on him and pin his ears to the sidewalk!"

"Boo, hiss!" said BoBo. "The Problem Solver's Club should never get violent."

"Can't we just sit down and have a talk with him?" asked Maria.

"He would steal our chair before we could sit down," Tony chimed in. "He stole my lunch at school Wednesday and fed it to the squirrels."

"Poor squirrels," BoBo sighed. "Did they live?"

"Verrrry funny," Tony said with a sour look. "At least I don't eat chocolate sundaes for breakfast!"

Maxi pounded the gavel to bring the meeting to order. "Let's keep on the subject of the new kid," he said importantly.

"I say let's be creative about this," Charlie said thoughtfully. "Suppose we first make a list of his problems."

"It would take all day!" Tony moaned.

"Shame on you, Tony." said Mini. "He's not THAT bad, is he? I have some paper and a pencil, and I'll write them down."

"OK, he's a lunch stealer," said Tony.

"So we need to help him with honesty," said Charlie.

"Great. Anyone have any honesty pills at home?" BoBo chimed in. "We'll poke a couple dozen down his throat."

"He lied to me the other day," said Pookie.

"That means he needs help with truthfulness," said Charlie.

"I've heard of truth serum," said Tony. "You pour it in a chocolate shake or something and make a kid drink it, and he has to tell the truth."

"Great idea," Pookie complained. "All we have to do is go to his house and feed him truth serum every morning for breakfast. Let's try another one!"

"Well, I heard him say some mean things to a friend of mine," Maria added.

"So, we need to help him with kindness," said Charlie. "You see, all we have to do is isolate all his problems and work on each one."

"What does isolate mean?" Pookie grumbled. "Keep it on our level, Charlie, so we'll know what's going on."

Charlie started to explain what *isolate* meant, but Maxi pounded the gavel on the orange crate again

to "keep it on the subject of the new kid."

"Wouldn't it be great if we could drag him down to a Problem Kid's Body Shop, like they do with cars," said BoBo. "They could just tear off the dishonesty piece and weld on a new honesty piece and then..."

"Hey, Maxi, pound that thing, and let's get back to the subject," said Pookie. "These wild ideas won't work."

"No, wait!" said Charlie. "BoBo has a good idea!"

"He DOES?" everyone said at once. Even BoBo looked startled.

"Yes, of course," said Charlie. "We have to decide first if we're going to repair this kid or replace him?"

"Replace him?" asked Maria. "You mean, like sell him or ship him off to a zoo?"

"No, but let's start first with the question of repair," said Charlie. "Is there anyone here who truly believes we can repair this kid with body shops or truth serums or honesty pills? If there is, stand up and tell us exactly how you will do it."

No one stood up, so Tony had a word to say. "I like the idea of replacing him, but we've got to have a better idea than shipping him to a zoo or selling him," he said. "Maybe we're really talking about remaking him."

"I have an idea," Mini said, jumping up. "We had a Bible story last Sunday in Sunday school. It told how Paul became a completely new person when he accepted Jesus."

"That's IT!" said Charlie.

"YEA!" shouted Pookie.

"BRAVO!" said Maria.

So The Problem Solver's Club all marched down the street to the new kid's house to invite him to Sunday school. And, as Maxi said, "We'll let Jesus do the job of remaking him."

LET'S TALK ABOUT THIS

What this story teaches: With all our ideas and inventions, we cannot truly remake a person ourselves, so we need Jesus to do that.

1. What kind of problem was The Problem Solver's Club trying to solve? What were some of the solutions that didn't work?

2. What was the right solution for the new kid? How would that work? Have you invited someone to Sunday school lately? How about this week?

Escape!

Acts 9: 23-25

Saul was a new man now. Everyone noticed the difference. Only a few days before, he had been a murderer. He had been filled with hatred for Jesus and His followers. Now he was one of them.

For several days Saul remained with Jesus' followers in Damascus. He didn't sit around all day, though, for Saul was busy preaching in the synagogues, the buildings where the Jewish people worshipped.

"Jesus is God's Son!" he proclaimed.

The people were amazed. Was this Saul the man who had left Jerusalem only a few days ago to hurt or kill the believers in Damascus? Was this Saul the man who violently argued that Jesus was not God's Son?

Now he was preaching in public that Jesus *was* God's Son. What had happened?

Saul told them about his meeting with Jesus on the road to Damascus. Nobody could argue with that. Nobody could tell Saul it hadn't happened, for several other men had been with him. They also had heard Jesus' voice.

The religious leaders in the synagogues were angry at Saul. They had planned to help him in his fight against Jesus' followers. Now Saul was making such a fight almost impossible. He was telling everyone that Jesus was alive, that He was God's Son, and that they should follow Him.

Although the religious leaders were angry at Saul, many of the people believed what he told them –

that he really had met Jesus on the way to Damascus and had heard His voice. They believed that Jesus was alive and in heaven. They also believed that Jesus was God's Son, the Savior, so they accepted Him and followed Him.

This made the religious leaders even more angry. "What can we do?" some asked.

"Kill Saul!" said others.

That was the answer. They would make plans to kill Saul as soon as possible. But their secret plans soon became known to the believers, who quickly told Saul.

"You must leave Damascus," they told him. "But you cannot go through the gates. The leaders have secret guards at every gate day and night now."

"How can we get Saul out of the city?" some of the believers asked.

Someone came up with a good idea. "A basket!" he said. "We'll let Saul down from the wall in a large basket."

Many people would have said that it was Saul's problem to get out of the city. But not the believers, Jesus' followers. Saul was one of them now, and

they would risk their lives to help him escape.

Late that night some believers went with Saul to the top of the city wall. Quietly they helped Saul into a large basket.

Someone whispered a prayer, and Saul's new friends quickly slid the basket over the wall and let it down to the ground below with a long rope.

Saul turned toward his new friends upon the wall, waved, and headed down the moonlit road toward Jerusalem.

"May God be with him," one of the believers whispered.

"He will!" said another. "God must surely have some wonderful plans for that man."

WHAT DO YOU THINK?
What this story teaches: Jesus' followers should help each other in times of trouble.
1. How might this story have been different if the believers had let Saul handle his escape by himself?
2. Why do you think the believers, Jesus' followers, risked their lives to help Saul escape? What did you learn from this about the way Christians should help each other?

A Tale of Three Muffkins

"Poppi, tell us a story," Mini and Maxi asked. This is the tale of three Muffkins that Poppi told:

Three Muffkins, Back, Jack, and Pack lived along a road in Muffkinland. Back lived a mile east of Jack, beside an old well where the three Muffkins got their water. Pack lived a mile west of Jack, where the three kept their corn in a storehouse. Jack lived by the largest tree in the forest.

Each day Back went two miles west to the storehouse to get his food, then walked two miles home. Pack went two miles east to the well to get his water, then walked two miles home. Jack walked a mile west to get his food, a mile home, then a mile east to get his water, and another mile home. The Muffkins did this for years, never thinking there was another way.

One day a wise old Muffkin came along the road and stopped at Jack's house for food and water. "I must first go to Back's well for water and then to Pack's storehouse for food."

"That's a four-mile trip!" said the wise old Muffkin. "I should have stopped at Pack's place for food and water instead."

"But he would have gone two miles to Back's well for water, then two miles home," said Jack. "That's still four miles!"

"Oh, dear, then I should go on to Back's well," said the wise old Muffkin. "That would be less trouble."

"No, it wouldn't," said Jack. "Back would still have to go four miles, two to Pack's storehouse and two home."

"There must be a better way," the wise old Muffkin said as he plopped on a big stump to think. Then he had a plan.

"Have you three Muffkins ever sat down together to see how you could help each other?" he asked.

"No, each does it his own way," said Jack.

Later, when Back passed by on the way to Pack's storehouse, the wise old Muffkin stopped him. Then when Pack passed by on the way to Back's well, the wise old Muffkin stopped him also.

"Now, let's all talk!" said the wise old Muffkin. But no one knew what to say, for each had always gone his own way. At last the wise old Muffkin spoke.

"I have a plan," said the wise old Muffkin. "Will you all follow it?" The three Muffkins nodded yes.

"Tomorrow Back will bring enough water here for Jack and Pack," said the wise old Muffkin. "Pack will bring enough food for Jack and Back. You will meet here at Jack's at nine o'clock. Back will walk two miles instead of four, and Pack will walk two miles instead of four."

"And Jack will not walk at all," said Back. "That's not fair."

"Listen to all of my plan," said the wise old Muffkin. "The next day Back will bring enough water for Jack and Pack. Pack will stay home, and Jack will bring Pack's water to his storehouse and then bring home enough food for himself and Back. So, Back and Jack will each walk two miles instead of four. Pack will not walk at all."

"What about me?" asked Back.

"On the third day, Pack will bring enough food to Jack for Back and Jack," said the wise old Muffkin. "He will wait while Jack takes Back's food to him and brings back enough water for himself and Pack. Then Pack will take his food home. Pack and Jack will each walk two miles instead of four, and Back will not walk at all."

Jack, Pack, and Back thought the plan was good, so they tried it. Before long, they learned how much fun it was to work together and how much more they got done by cutting their walking time in half. Later, they invented something to carry the food and water. To show how much they liked working together, they named it "Jack's Back Pack."

LET'S TALK ABOUT THIS

What this story teaches: Jesus' followers can do more and better work, and enjoy it more, by working together.

1. What did the Muffkins learn about working together? Why is this important? Why is it especially important for Christians?

2. Why is it better for family members to work together instead of each going his own way? Why is it better for people in a church to work together? What would Jesus want?

Jacob-The Man Who Left Home

A Sad Day for Jacob's Family

Genesis 27; 28: 1-9

"I am here, father," Esau announced.

Isaac, almost blind now, sat alone in his tent. He motioned for Esau to come in and sit near him.

"I am an old man, now," Isaac began. "Who knows how much longer I will live? It is time to give you my blessing. Then the birthright will be yours for sure."

Esau smiled. He remembered that day many years before when his younger twin brother Jacob had "bought" that birthright for a bowl of lentil soup. Esau had cursed the day, and his brother, many times since. He had worried often, afraid that he might have lost the birthright. With it, he would lose the right to lead the family and receive most of his father's property after he died.

"Take your bow and arrows and find a deer for me," Isaac continued. "Cook it the way I like it, and bring it here for me to eat. Then I will bless you before I die."

Esau rushed from the tent. He must hurry, for he was anxious now to settle this. As soon as his father spoke the words of "the blessing" to him, the birthright was his forever. No one could take it from him.

Esau would have hurried even faster if he had seen his mother Rebekah hiding behind Isaac's tent. She had heard every word that Isaac had said.

"Listen carefully," Rebekah told Jacob when she found him. "Bring me two young goats, and I will cook them the way your father likes his meat. Pretend that you are Esau, and he will give you the blessing."

"But what if he finds out what we are doing?" Jacob argued. "He will give me a curse instead of a blessing."

"Then I will accept the curse instead of you," said Rebekah. "Now go. There is no time to lose."

Jacob knew that there wasn't much time. Even now, Esau was looking for the deer in the fields.

Rebekah hurried, too. While the young goats were cooking in the pot, she fastened their hairy skins to Jacob's hands, arms, and neck.

At last everything was ready. Jacob carried the meat to his father's tent and placed it before him.

"Here is the meat, father," Jacob said, trying to sound as much like Esau as possible.

"Who are you?" Isaac said, almost startled by Jacob's sudden appearance. Isaac was so blind that he could not see who was there.

"I'm Esau," Jacob lied. "Your meat is ready for you to eat."

Old Isaac was suspicious now. "How did you find the meat so quickly?" he asked.

"The Lord helped me," Jacob lied again. Jacob felt uncomfortable when he lied a second time to his father. He felt even more uncomfortable because he had lied about the Lord.

"Come, let me feel you," said Isaac. "Then I will know if you are Esau."

Isaac's fingers moved over Jacob's hands and arms. They felt the goat's hair that Rebekah had put there and on Jacob's neck. Jacob must have trembled as his father slowly and suspiciously touched him.

"Your voice sounds like Jacob, but you feel like Esau," Isaac murmured. "Are you REALLY Esau?"

Jacob must have felt like running from the tent. To lie to one's father was a terrible wrong. To lie about the Lord was even worse. Now, Jacob was in a corner. If he said no, his father would put a curse upon him. Two lies forced him to tell a third.

"Yes, I am Esau," he said at last.

Jacob watched nervously as his father slowly ate the meat he had brought. He was even more nervous as he bowed before his father and heard him give the blessing to him. The blessing made Jacob head over the family after Isaac died. It gave Jacob most of the family possessions.

Then Jacob quickly left.

Soon after, Esau came with his meat. "Eat my meat, and then bless me," Esau said.

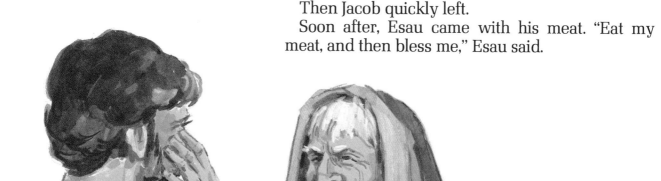

Old Isaac sat up in his bed. "Who are you?" he demanded.

Esau was stunned. "I am Esau," he said. "You wanted to bless me."

Isaac began to tremble. "Then who was just here?" he asked. "I already blessed him and put him over you and your family. I cannot take that blessing away."

When Esau heard that, he began to cry. Once more, Jacob had stolen his birthright. So Esau hated Jacob for what he did. "I'll kill him," he cried out.

As Isaac lay down on his bed once more, he must have thought many times about Jacob's three lies. He, like Esau, must have cried.

It was a sad day for Jacob's family, for the family was torn apart. For twenty years Jacob would live away from his family, dreading the day he would meet his brother or father again.

WHAT DO YOU THINK?

What this story teaches: Lies can tear a family apart. Lies about the Lord hurt Him and us.

1. Why did Jacob tell a lie to his father? Why was he forced to tell a second and third lie? Why didn't he stop with the first one?

2. What did Jacob's lies do to his family? What do you think they did to him?

The Paper Family

Maxi and Mini watched closely as Poppi folded the sheet of paper once, then folded it again. "What are you doing?" they asked.

"You'll see!" said Poppi, as he cut a tall upside-down V from the bottom to the center of the folded paper. Maxi and Mini came closer as Poppi cut a big notch on the left side, another on the right, and then a circle near the top.

"Now watch this," said Poppi as he put down the scissors. Poppi carefully unfolded the paper and there were four paper people with hands joined.

"Wow! I've never seen that done before," said Mini. "That's neat. Just look how their hands and feet are together!"

"This is The Paper Family," said Poppi. "Say hello to them."

Maxi felt a little strange saying hello to some paper people, but he managed to mumble something. Mini chimed in with a bright sunny hello, and Mommi joined in with a laugh.

"Now, we're going to name them," said Poppi. "This one is Isaac." Then Poppi wrote ISAAC on the first paper person.

On the next paper person he wrote REBEKAH, on the third, ESAU, and on the last, JACOB.

"Those are the four people in the Bible story you just read," said Maxi.

But before Maxi and Mini knew what was happening, Poppi ripped the fourth person from the others and threw it across the table. "POPPI!" Mini gasped. "What are you doing?"

"That's the first lie!" Poppi said. Then he ripped off the third paper person from the others and threw it on another side of the table. "And that's the second."

Maxi and Mini were shocked to see what Poppi was doing. "What is it?" they begged.

But Poppi didn't answer. Instead, he ripped the other two paper people apart and threw one on each empty side of the table. "That's the third lie!" he said. "And that takes care of that paper family!"

"But Poppi, are you all right?" Maxi asked. Mini stared at Poppi, almost not knowing what to think.

"Yes, I'm all right," said Poppi. "But those three lies certainly fixed that paper family, didn't they?"

"But WHY?" Mini begged. "Why did you do it?"

"To help you see what happened to Jacob's real family," said Poppi. "One lie, then two, then three, and the family was torn apart, just like our paper family. Jacob went far away, Esau went later, and Isaac and Rebekah were torn apart in a way that your Mommi and I would certainly never want to be."

Maxi smiled. "OK, I see," he said.

"Me, too," said Mini. "But you had us worried for a while. May I keep The Paper Family?"

"Of course, Mini," said Poppi. "But why do you want them?"

"I'll tape them together and hang them on my wall," said Mini. "They will remind me not to tell lies to my family, for I certainly don't want us ripped apart like that!"

LET'S TALK ABOUT THIS

What this story teaches: Lies can tear your family apart, just as they did Jacob's family.

1. Why did Mini want the torn paper people? What would they help her remember?

2. How did lies tear Jacob's family apart? How could they tear your family apart? What would the Lord want you to do?

Stairway to Heaven

Genesis 28: 10-22

Jacob's family was in trouble. His father, Issac, sat alone in his tent, a deceived, broken old man. Blind and bedfast with old age, Isaac heard Jacob's lies again and again in his mind. "I am Esau." "The Lord helped me get this meat." "Yes, I AM Esau."

There was a deep hurt in Isaac's heart that only time would heal. More important, Isaac suddenly had bitter suspicions about Jacob, and only time would heal those.

Esau was furious with Jacob. He had vowed to kill his brother as soon as Isaac died.

Jacob and his mother, Rebekah, were afraid that Esau would kill Jacob. So they made plans for the only thing that could be done. Jacob must leave home and family and not return until the whole family would welcome each other again.

"You don't want Jacob to marry these foreign girls around here, do you?" Rebekah asked Isaac.

Of course he didn't, so Isaac gave his approval for Jacob to leave. Jacob would go far to the north to marry a wife among his distant relatives at Haran.

As soon as he had packed his few possessions and supplies for the trip on some family camels, Jacob headed northward toward Haran. He said good-bye to his family and friends. As he mounted the camel, he glanced back for one last look at his mother, Rebekah, who alone had come to see him off. It was the last time he would see her. Then Jacob left Beer-sheba with a sad, sorry feeling filling his heart.

As evening approached, Jacob set up camp on a lonely hillside. With his mind whirling, filled with thoughts of home and family, Jacob ate and lay down to sleep. There was no bed tonight for Jacob—only a rock for a pillow and the stars above for his tent.

In his dreams that night, Jacob saw something like a stairway or ladder. It went up higher and higher through the most faraway stars until it reached into heaven. Angels walked up and down between heaven and earth.

The Lord stood at the top of this stairway, calling down to Jacob. "I am the Lord," He said. "I am the God of your grandfather, Abraham, and your father, Isaac. I am giving the land where you sleep to you, your children, and to their children for many, many years. There will be many thousands of your descendants, and they will go to all parts of the earth."

The Lord said also to Jacob, "I will go with you on your journey. I will take you safely there and back to this place."

Jacob woke up suddenly. The stairway was gone. The angels were gone. Only the night stars twinkled in the sky above him.

"This is God's home!" he cried out. "It is the doorway to heaven!"

When morning came Jacob turned his stone pillow on end and poured some olive oil on it. "From now on, this place will be called Bethel," said Jacob. The name *Bethel* meant "the House of God," for Jacob had said that this was God's home.

Jacob made this vow to the Lord God: "If You will go with me, protect me, give me food and clothing, and bring me safely back home to Beer-sheba, I will worship You only as my God. This stone will be an altar where I will worship You, and I will give You back a tenth of all You give me."

After his prayer, Jacob stood quietly looking into the sky. He remembered his dream and the words God had spoken to him.

Then Jacob mounted his camel and headed north again toward Haran and a new life. But the journey was different now, for God was with him as He had promised.

WHAT DO YOU THINK?
What this story teaches: The Lord wants to go with us wherever we go, but He also wants us to invite Him.
1. What did the Lord say to Jacob in his dream? Why was this so important to Jacob as he went to a strange land far away?
2. What did Jacob say to the Lord in his prayer? Why was this important to the Lord?
3. Do you think the Lord went with Jacob on the rest of his journey? What makes you think so?

The Police Station

"Maxi!"

"Wha...what?" Maxi stammered. "I'm sorry, Poppi. Were you talking to me?"

"Earth to Maxi," said Poppi. "Are you there?"

"I...I was just thinking," said Maxi.

"Wonderful!" said Poppi cheerfully. "That's a good thing to do at least once each day. It keeps our engines in tune."

"I'm sorry, Poppi," Maxi said glumly. "I'm just not in a joking mood."

"Something you want to tell me?"

"I...well, I guess not."

"Something you want to ask me?"

Maxi was silent for a moment or two. "What should someone do if he has to do something difficult, and he needs help, but he doesn't really know if he should ask for it?"

"What kind of help?" Poppi asked.

"Well, this person has to go to the police station," Maxi said softly.

"Sounds like he's in real trouble," said Poppi, trying to look calm.

"He is!"

"Sounds like this person in trouble needs a friend," said Poppi.

"He does!"

"A bigger friend?"

"Yes!"

"To go with him?"

"How did you know?"

"I was a boy once, Maxi. But why doesn't this boy, er, this person in trouble, just ask the bigger friend?"

"Perhaps he's afraid to bother him, or not sure if he should bother him. Or he might not be sure if the bigger friend would want to go with him."

Poppi smiled. "Does this person in trouble really WANT the bigger friend to go?"

"Yes."

"Well, then," said Poppi, "if the friend in trouble really WANTS the bigger friend to go with him, and the bigger friend really WANTS to go, there's just one thing left to do."

"What's that?"

"Ask!"

"Will you?"

"Of course, let's go!" said Poppi. "But what did you do?"

"Do? I didn't do anything," said Maxi. "I just have to ask the police chief some questions for a paper I'm doing for social studies."

"Is that all?" asked Poppi.

"Yes."

"Whew!"

LET'S TALK ABOUT THIS

What this story teaches: Just as the Lord wants to go with us when we need help, so poppis and mommis want to go with their children when they need help. But it is nice to ask.

1. Why do you think Maxi was afraid to go alone to the police station? Would you have been? Why was he afraid to ask Poppi to go with him?

2. Did Poppi really want to go? Does the Lord want to go with us when we need help? How does this remind you of the Lord's going with Jacob on his journey?

A New Home for Jacob

Genesis 29: 1-14

After his dream at Bethel, Jacob traveled toward Haran. Along the way he wondered about his mother's childhood home and her family there. What would her brother, Laban, be like? Would he meet him? Would he and his family still be alive?

"Perhaps they have moved on to some other place," Jacob may have thought. "And if they have, how shall I find them?"

At last, after several days, Jacob arrived in the broad, flat pasturelands near Haran. This was the land of his mother, Rebekah, and her brother, Laban.

In the distance, Jacob saw a well. Three flocks of sheep lay nearby, waiting to be watered. The well had a heavy stone over it, and the shepherds sat near it talking.

"Which city do you live in?" Jacob asked the shepherds.

"Haran," they answered.

"Then you must know Laban?" Jacob asked.

"Of course," they said. "We know him."

"Is he well?" Jacob continued.

"Yes, he is," said the shepherds. "See that shepherd girl coming with her sheep? That's his daughter Rachel."

Jacob stood, quietly watching the beautiful Rachel as she brought her sheep to the well. Could this be the girl he would marry?

More than anything else, Jacob wanted to be alone with Rachel at this moment. If only he could get the shepherds to leave.

"What are you waiting for?" Jacob asked, almost forgetting to be polite. "You should water your sheep so you can take them back to pasture."

The shepherds laughed. "We don't do it that way," they said. "When all of the shepherds have brought their sheep, then we roll the stone away and water the sheep at one time."

Jacob didn't care what they usually did. He hurried over to the well, rolled away the stone, and poured water for Rachel's sheep. Imagine how surprised she was to see him do that!

Jacob cried as he kissed Rachel and told her that they were cousins, that his mother, Rebekah, was Rachel's aunt, and that her father, Laban, was Jacob's uncle.

Rachel was so excited that she left her sheep there at the well and ran all the way home. Before long, Laban ran back to the well with her. He hugged Jacob several times. "Just think!" he exclaimed. "You are my sister Rebekah's son!"

Jacob must have remembered now the Lord's promise to go with him and lead him. He must have silently thanked the Lord for leading him so quickly to his relatives. Here he would be safe and would have a place to stay until the day when he could go home to Beer-sheba.

WHAT DO YOU THINK?
What this story teaches: The Lord will give His people a home away from home when they need it.
1. Why did Jacob run away from his father's home at Beer-sheba? Why did he come here to Haran?
2. How did the Lord show that He was with Jacob as he arrived in Haran? What did He do for Jacob?

In the Land of Muffkins

A Muffin Make-believe Story

"We're so glad you came with us to the library," said Maxi. "You know what these books are about, and Mini and I don't."

"I know some of them," said Mommi. "And I will be happy to help you two find some extra summer reading."

It really was fun to go library exploring together. It was especially fun when Mommi knew what the book was about and whether she thought Maxi or Mini would enjoy it.

Mommi and Mini were looking at some books in the horse story section when they heard Maxi whistle and say, "Wow," at least two or three times. "Find something interesting?" Mommi asked.

Maxi brought a book over for Mommi and Mini to see. "Look at that giant!" he said. "And all those people holding him to the ground with ropes!"

"Oh, that's *Gulliver's Travels*," said Mommi. "The giant really isn't a giant, but a Poppi-size man. The other people are mouse-size."

"Mouse-size people," Maxi whispered. He sat down at a library table and stared at the painting on the cover of the book for a long time, while Mommi told how Dr. Gulliver was shipwrecked on this island and how the mouse-size people finally gave him a home away from his real home in England.

Maxi was still thinking about Gulliver and the mouse-size people when he went to bed that night. When he fell asleep at last, he dreamed that he was in a terrible storm at sea in an old sailing ship. At last the ship was wrecked, and he made it safely to the shore of a strange land.

Exhausted from the shipwreck, Maxi Gulliver fell asleep on the beach. But when he awoke in the morning, he was tied to the beach with many small ropes. Standing nearby were a number of mouse-like creatures.

"Who...who are you?" Maxi Gulliver asked.

"We're Muffkins," said their king. "But you should have let us ask first who you are."

Then Maxi Gulliver told the Muffkins about his shipwreck and how he made it safely to their land on some planks from the ship. "I'm your friend," said Maxi Gulliver. "Please give me a home away from home."

"Perhaps we will," said the Muffkin king. But first he sent a scouting party along the beach to search for pieces from the wrecked ship. Before long the scouts returned.

"Maxi Gulliver is right," they said. "There are many pieces from a shipwreck along the beach."

"Welcome to the land of Muffkins," said the Muffkin king. Then he gave the royal command for the ropes to be cut and Maxi Gulliver to be set free.

"You may live with us at the royal castle," said the king.

But when Maxi Gulliver saw the royal castle, he smiled. "It's like a dollhouse," he said. "I can't live in there."

Then the Muffkins showed Maxi Gulliver a great cave not far from the castle. "It isn't much now," they said. "But we will help you fix it so that it will be home away from home."

Maxi Gulliver looked at the cave. The Muffkins were right. It could be fixed up nice. But it would never be warm and bright like his beautiful room back home.

"Thank you for making me welcome in the land of Muffkins," said Maxi Gulliver. "And I am grateful for this cave where I can sleep."

That night Maxi Gulliver lay down in the cave to sleep. He thought of the kind way the Muffkins had helped him find a home away from home. But he dreamed of his home back home. He dreamed that he found a boat in the land of the Muffkins and set sail toward his real home.

Then Maxi Gulliver heard someone calling. It was time to get up. He opened his eyes, and when he looked around, he was back in his own room again. A home away from home was nice, but not nearly as nice as his home at home!

LET'S TALK ABOUT THIS

What this story teaches: Even though a home away from home will never be as nice for us as a home at home, we should appreciate it when others provide that home away from home for us.

1. How was Maxi Gulliver like Jacob at Haran? How was he like Gulliver in the book?

2. Has someone ever given you a home away from home? Did you thank him for it? Have you and your parents ever given someone else a home away from home? Was he grateful?

3. How is the world in which we live like a home away from our "forever" home in heaven?

My Way

Matthew 21: 33-46

Jesus always had trouble with the people called Pharisees. They thought that they were doing God's work. But they would not do it the way God wanted it done. Instead, each wanted to do it "my way."

Jesus tried to tell them how God wanted His work done. He tried to tell them that He was God's Son and had lived with God in heaven, so He knew what God wanted. But whenever He tried to tell them, they became angry and wanted to kill Him. They would not believe what He said.

So Jesus told them this story:

There was once a man who bought some land and planted a vineyard. He worked hard to make this the most wonderful vineyard of all. He planted vines and hedges, pulled weeds, and built stone fences. He even built a watchtower where guards could make sure no one would steal his grapes.

One day the man had to go away to another land. He told some servants they would become the caretakers of his vineyard. They would make sure that His work was done.

As the grapes grew ripe, the vineyard owner chose some other servants to gather them. He sent them to his vineyard to do this special work for him. But when they arrived, the caretakers were angry. They thought they were in charge of the vineyard. They did not want to do things the way the owner wanted. Instead each wanted to do the work "my way."

The caretakers beat one of those good servants whom the owner had chosen to do his work. They threw stones at another and killed another.

Naturally the owner was surprised and hurt. He had put those caretakers in charge of his vineyard. But he expected them to do things his way, not theirs.

The owner chose more servants to gather his grapes and sent them to his vineyard. This time the caretakers were waiting, ready to jump on them. They beat some, threw stones at others, and killed others.

The owner was shocked when he heard about that. How could those wicked caretakers do such a thing? The vineyard was his, not theirs. He could

do with it as he wished. The good servants who came to gather grapes were obeying him, not the caretakers. The caretakers did not want to do things the way the owner wanted. But what should he do?

"I will send my son to gather my grapes," he said. "No one would dare hurt the owner's son!"

But they did. When the caretakers saw the son coming, they began to whisper among themselves.

"What will we do?" some asked.

"Kill him!" said others. "He is the owner's son, so he will get this vineyard when the owner dies. Let's kill him now and take the vineyard for our own. It is the only way we can keep doing things our way."

That is what they did. They dragged the owner's son from the vineyard and killed him.

As He finished the story, Jesus looked closely at the men who pretended to do God's work. "What will the vineyard owner do when he comes?" He asked.

"Put those wicked caretakers to death in some horrible way!" the men answered. "Then he will choose someone else, who will do his work the way he wants."

"You are those caretakers!" Jesus said. "God is the owner of the vineyard. Since you won't do His work the way He wants, He will take it away from you and give it to others."

The Pharisees were angry. They would have killed Jesus at that very moment, but the people nearby were His friends and would not let them. For once, not one of them could do things "my way."

WHAT DO YOU THINK?

What this story teaches: God wants people to do His work the way He wants, not the way they want. If they don't, He will take that work away and give it to others.

1. Did the caretakers in the story want to do the owner's work his way or theirs? How was this like the men to whom Jesus was telling the story? Did they want to do God's work His way or "my way"?

2. What happened to the wicked caretakers? What did Jesus say would happen to the Pharisees? What happens to those who pretend to do God's work but will only do it "my way"?

The Royal Trumpet Tooter

"Hear ye! Hear ye!" the king of the Muffkins proclaimed. "I will choose a royal trumpet tooter today. Whenever I have a special message to give to the people, he will give a loud and long toot on his trumpet."

"Wow!" said all of the trumpet tooters of the land. "That is wonderful work!"

"The royal trumpet tooter lives in the palace!" said one.

"He toots on a golden trumpet!" said another.

"He eats fine food."

"And wears fine clothes."

"And everyone looks at him and says, 'He works for the king! He is special.'"

All the trumpet tooters in Muffkinland came to the palace to toot for the king. Each wanted to become the royal trumpet tooter and

live in the palace,
toot a golden trumpet,
eat fine food,
wear fine clothes, and
have everyone say he was special, for
he worked for the king.

You have never heard so much tooting in all your life. The king of the Muffkins had never heard so much tooting in his life either.

One went toot-ta-toot-ta-toot-ta-toot.

Another went toot-ta-ta-toot-ta-ta.

And another went toot-toot-ta-toot.

At last the king of the Muffkins chose the toot-toot-ta-toot. He told that trumpet tooter he could

live in the palace,
toot a golden trumpet,
eat fine food,
wear fine clothes, and
have everyone say he was special, for
he worked for the king.

Of course, the new royal trumpet tooter was the happiest trumpet tooter in the land. He
  moved to the palace,
  tooted on the king's golden trumpet,
  ate the king's fine food,
  wore the king's fine clothes, and
  had everyone say he was special, for
  he worked for the king.

But there was a problem. The new royal trumpet tooter grew tired of toot-toot-ta-toot. Soon he went toot-ta-ta-ta-toot-ta-ta-ta.

"Stop! Stop!" shouted the king of the Muffkins. "I want toot-toot-ta-toot."

"And I want toot-ta-ta-ta-toot-ta-ta-ta," said the royal trumpet tooter. "I am the royal trumpet tooter, not you."

The king of the Muffkins was angry, but he said nothing more, until he saw the royal trumpet tooter tooting on his old tin horn, not the king's golden trumpet.

"Stop! Stop!" shouted the king of the Muffkins. "I want my golden trumpet tooted, not your old tin horn."

"And I want to toot my old tin horn," said the royal trumpet tooter. "I am the royal trumpet tooter, not you."

The king of the Muffkins was angry, but he said nothing more until he saw the royal trumpet tooter tooting in some silly looking old clothes, not the beautiful clothes that the king had given him.

"Stop! Stop!" said the king of the Muffkins. "You must toot in the royal clothes I gave you, not in those silly old clothes you brought."

"And I want to toot in these old clothes," said the royal trumpet tooter. "I am the royal trumpet tooter, not you."

This time the king of the Muffkins was very angry. He also said something. "Get out!" he told the royal trumpet tooter. "I am the king. You WERE the royal trumpet tooter. Now I will find another who will go toot-toot-ta-toot on my golden trumpet in the royal clothes I give him."

So the foolish tooter had to
leave the king's palace and go back to his hut, give up the golden trumpet and toot on his old
    tin horn,
stop eating the king's fine food,
stop wearing the king's fine clothes, and
nobody said he was special now, for
he no longer worked for the king.

LET'S TALK ABOUT THIS
What this story teaches: God, and kings, want us to do their work as they choose, and not "my way."
1. Why did all the trumpet tooters want to become the royal trumpet tooter?
2. What happened to the royal trumpet tooter who was chosen? Why did the king take his job away from him?
3. When God gives you work to do, should you do it His way, or your way? What happens if you keep on telling God, "MY way"?

Ten Girls Who Went to a Wedding

Matthew 25: 1-13

Jesus told a story about an evening wedding with ten bridesmaids. At first, they were to wait outside the bride's home until the bridegroom came with his friends. Then, with lamps lit, they would join the wedding procession and return to the bridegroom's home for the wedding feast.

But something went wrong. The bridegroom did not come at the time he was expected. So the ten girls sat down to wait.

Five of the girls had brought extra oil for their lamps. They knew that bridegrooms sometimes did not come as soon as they were expected. People in Jesus' time did not have clocks or watches, so they would not ask people to come at eight o'clock or six-thirty. The wedding would be held just sometime that night.

The other five girls knew this too. But they foolishly came with only enough oil to fill their lamps. What a careless, thoughtless thing to do!

Hours passed and still the bridegroom had not appeared. One by one the girls fell asleep while

their lamps still burned. One by one their lamps began to sputter and then went out.

At midnight one girl woke suddenly. Far down the street she heard the bridegroom and his friends coming with music and singing. In a few minutes he would reach the bride's home.

"Wake up! Wake up!" the girl shouted. "The bridegroom is coming!"

The other girls jumped up and trimmed off the burnt part of the wicks in their clay lamps. Then they noticed that their lamps had burned all of the olive oil in them.

The five girls who had brought more oil put it in their lamps. But the other five girls had no oil.

"Give us some of yours," they begged.

"We can't do that," the girls said as they lit their lamps again. "You know that we have only enough for our own lamps."

The five who had not brought more oil knew this was true. But what could they do?

"Run to the shops," someone suggested. "Perhaps one is still open and you can buy oil there."

"At midnight?" one of the unprepared girls asked.

But there really was no other way, so the five foolish, unprepared girls ran down the dark street.

They could not go into the wedding without lighted lamps.

While they were gone, the bridegroom came to receive his bride. What a happy, excited group of friends came with him. Some sang. Others played musical instruments. The rest shouted and joked with each other.

The five girls waited while the bride and her parents came out. The bride's parents presented her to the bridegroom with their blessing, then everyone shouted, sang, and played instruments even louder than before.

The bride, her parents, the five bridesmaids with lighted lamps, and the bride's friends joined the bridegroom and his friends. They all made their way through the streets to the bridegroom's house. There the wedding would be finished, and a great feast would be held.

As soon as the last guest was inside, the door was bolted. No one could come in after that.

Somewhere in the late hours of the night the other five girls returned. They had found oil, trimmed their lamps, and wanted to join the wedding feast. But no one would let them in.

"Go away," the master of the feast called out. "You are too late. You know you can't come in now. How do we know you belong here? Go away!"

Sad and sorry, the five girls made their way home through the sleepy village. The farther they went, the less they heard the happy sounds of the wedding feast. At last they turned down one dark street toward their homes, and they heard the happy sounds no more.

These five sorry girls had known all the time that they might need more oil. They simply did not bring it. No one knows why. Perhaps they were lazy, or thought they knew more than others, or were just foolish.

But we do know that they never got to the wedding. Instead, they had only the dark streets of the village.

WHAT DO YOU THINK?
What this story teaches: It is wise to prepare early for the time when Jesus returns to earth or the time when we go to meet Him.

1. What happened to the five wise girls who prepared for the bridegroom to come late? What happened to the five foolish girls who did not?

2. What did you learn about preparing early for something important? How can we best prepare for the time when Jesus comes back to earth, or for the time when we must die and meet Him face to face? Have you accepted Him yet as your Savior?

Get Ready

"Mini, would you like to earn some extra money this afternoon?" Mommi asked.

Mini clapped her hands. "Oh, yes," she said. "I have been dreaming about some things in the catalog. This will help me buy one of them."

"Good, then I would like for you to vacuum the house for me," said Mommi. "I will pay you five dollars. But you must do a thorough job, and you must do it by two thirty. My Bible study group meets here at three and I MUST do some shopping before then."

"I'll do it!" said Mini.

"Five dollars!" Mini squealed when Mommi had gone. "Five dollars! I can hardly believe it. Think of the things that will help me get."

Mini was thinking so much of the things that she ran to find the catalog. Then she plopped down in a big chair "for just a minute" to thumb through it.

Mini started in the clothing section. She counted how much more she would need to earn for each item, and how much she had, and how much Mommi would pay.

Then she turned to the game and toy section and did the same for it. Mini became so interested in the catalog that she completely forgot about time.

Suddenly Mini heard the door close. Who was that? Poppi was at work. Maxi was at a ball game. Mini looked up from the catalog slowly to see Mommi standing in the doorway.

"All finished?" Mommi asked cheerfully.

Mini stared at Mommi, then at the catalog, then at the clock on the wall. It was exactly two thirty. But how could it be? It wasn't possible. She stared at the clock again, and it WAS two thirty. Then she looked back at the catalog in her hands, and then at Mommi again.

Mini began to cry and threw herself into Mommi's arms. Then she told Mommi what had happened. "I got into other things and just wasn't ready for you to come home yet," she sniffed.

"I can't pay you for work you didn't do, Mini," Mommi said softly, "You know that. But I think you learned something worth more than the five dollars."

"What is that?" Mini sniffed.

"To be SURE to be ready when something important is about to happen," Mommi answered. "Do you remember the Bible story of the five wise and five foolish bridesmaids at the wedding? Our Bible study this afternoon is about that. You may sit with us if you like. Five girls got interested in other things and 'forgot' to get ready for the wedding, and they were bridesmaids!"

"But what important thing should I get ready for?" Mini asked. "What does this have to do with me?"

Mommi gave Mini a big hug. "Not just you. All of us!" she said. "Some day each of us will die and go to meet Jesus. Or He may come to earth first to meet us. We don't know when either will be, so we must get ready by accepting Him as our Savior. We also must get ready by living for Him each day as we should."

"I have accepted Him as my Savior," said Mini. "So I'm ready that way. But I'm going to put a little note on my mirror that says GET READY. Then each morning I will not only get ready for school, but I'll read my Bible and pray and get ready for Jesus."

"Good," said Mommi. "But now I must get ready for my Bible group." So Mommi went to get things ready, and Mini ran to help her.

LET'S TALK ABOUT THIS

What this story teaches: We must each get ready to meet Jesus, whether we go to meet Him or He comes first to meet us.

1. Was Mini ready for Mommi when she returned? Why not? Do you sometimes let other things keep you from getting ready for something important?

2. Are you ready to meet Jesus?

A Story About Talents

Matthew 25: 14-30

Soon Jesus must leave earth to return to His home in heaven. While He was gone, His followers would be in charge of His work on earth. He must help them understand how to use time and talents wisely so that His work would be done. This was a story He told to help them understand.

One day a merchant called three servants to a meeting. "I must go far away to another country," the merchant said. "While I am gone, you must be in charge of my work."

The merchant gave one servant five talents of gold, worth many thousands of dollars. He gave a second servant two talents of gold, also worth many thousands of dollars. Then he gave the third servant one talent of gold.

"Invest these talents wisely," said the merchant. Then he left.

Early the next morning the man with five talents went to work. He bought, sold, and traded. In time, the five talents were worth ten talents.

The servant with two talents also bought and sold and traded until his two talents were worth four. But the servant with one talent was not like the other two. He was afraid to buy and sell and trade. He was also lazy. So he dug a hole and hid the gold in it. Then he went home to sleep.

"Look at those two," he often said as he saw the other servants hurrying here and there, buying and selling and trading. "They work hard all day. For what? To make our master rich! Not me. I want to enjoy life."

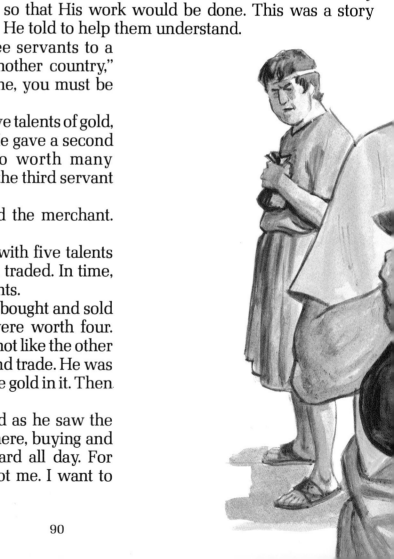

One day a meeting of the three servants was called suddenly. The master had returned and wanted to know how his servants had invested his talents.

The servants brought their gold to the master. The first one stepped forward. "You left five talents of gold with me," he said. "I have bought, sold, and traded. Today I have ten talents to give to you."

"You have been a good and faithful servant," said the master. "Now I will promote you into a better job, for I know that you will do well with it."

The next servant stepped forward with four talents of gold. "You gave me two to invest, and I also have doubled your money for you," he told the master.

"You also are a good and faithful servant," said the master. "I will promote you into a better job, for I know that you will do well with it."

The third servant placed the one talent before his master. "Here is your talent back," he said. "Nothing is lost. It's all here."

"But nothing is gained, either," the master answered. "If you were too lazy to work, you could have taken it to a bank. It would have earned some interest."

The master ordered someone to take the one talent from that man and give it to the one with ten. He would use it wisely.

"Now get that lazy man out of my sight," he ordered.

Two servants were promoted into power and honor. The third was sent away with nothing. Jesus was telling us all that we must wisely use our talents, time, and money for Him. To do so brings power and honor. To fail leaves us empty-handed.

WHAT DO YOU THINK?
What this story teaches: We must either use, or lose, the talents and gifts God gives us.
1. What did you learn about being a good servant for Jesus?
2. What kind of talents does God give us? What does He expect us to do with them?

Rusty, Rotten Treasure

"Do you call this a treasure hunt?" Pookie complained. "Look at this list!"

"A rusty piece of iron," Maria giggled.

"A rotten board," Tony said with a smirk on his face. "If I get enough of this kind of treasure, I can start a junk pile."

"Moldy bread," BoBo read. "Come on, Maxi, are you serious about all this?"

"I detect a plot," Charlie added. "Maxi has something on his mind."

"Yeah," Pookie said. "Rusty iron, rotten boards, and moldy bread. Can't you see those things rattling around up there?"

"OK, the treasure hunt will begin," said Maxi, ignoring all the friendly comments. "Let's go."

"First one to the city dump wins," BoBo shouted.

"If it weren't so far, that really wouldn't be a bad idea," Charlie added. "But I still think Maxi has something on his mind."

"Do you?" Mini asked when the others had left for the treasure hunt and she had stayed behind to put refreshments on the table.

"Perhaps," said Maxi. "We'll see."

BoBo was back first with the rusty piece of iron, the rotten board, and the moldy bread. In fact, he

was fifteen minutes earlier than Charlie, who complained that moldy bread was too hard to find and that any person who found it deserved to win.

Pookie had a rusty nail and a rotten piece of tree limb, but the others grumbled that a tree limb was not a board and therefore it didn't count. Pookie didn't like that, so he questioned BoBo's moldy bread. Everyone looked close and found that it really wasn't moldy, but just touched up with a little green paint.

"See!" said Charlie. "I told you it's too hard to find moldy bread."

Tony was the last person in, after Maria, who had decided that it was stupid to look for old pieces of junk and had gone home for a sandwich. He had a rusty hinge and a rotten board from an old gate his father had thrown behind their garage several years before, even before Tony was born! "And I even have a piece of moldy bread," he said triumphantly.

"OK, where did you get it?" Charlie demanded.

Tony tried to change the subject, but everyone demanded that he tell. "I made a picnic lunch two weeks ago and forgot to take it, so it was moldy," Tony finally admitted. "We were going to throw it out but forgot."

"YUK," some of them said.

"OK, now we have brought the city dump to Maxi's house," Charlie said sarcastically. "What's it all about, Maxi?"

"Our Bible study," Maxi said coolly.

"BIBLE STUDY?" several asked. "How?"

"Now that I have your attention, sit down and listen," Maxi added. Then Maxi told the Bible story about the talents.

"But that was gold, not rotten boards and rusty hinges," said Pookie.

"Not really," said Maxi. "The story is about using the good things God gives us, or losing them. The hinge is rusty because it wasn't used and kept clean. The boards are rotten because they haven't been painted and kept in use. And Tony's lunch bread got moldy because he didn't eat it, which is what lunches are for."

"Not bad," said BoBo. "Really, that's not bad!"

"I told you Maxi had something on his mind," said Charlie.

"Right. Rusty hinges, rotten boards, and moldy bread," added Pookie.

Everyone laughed, but all agreed that they would always think of using God's gifts when they saw any rusty, rotten treasure lying around.

LET'S TALK ABOUT THIS
What this story teaches: God gives us many wonderful gifts, but we will lose them if we do not use them for Him.

1. What did Maxi's friends learn from the rusty, rotten treasure? What did you learn?

2. Make a list of some of the gifts that God has given you. Beside each one, write how you are using that gift. Are there some you are not using well? Remember, you may lose them if you do not use them.

Mini's Word List

Twelve words that all Minis and Maxis want to know:

ARK–Two kinds of ark are mentioned in the Bible. Noah's ark was a large boat. The Ark mentioned in this book was a golden chest that the people of Israel carried in the wilderness. In the promised land, they placed it in the Tabernacle, then in the Temple. This chest contained the stones on which the Ten Commandments were written.

BIRTHRIGHT–In Bible times the oldest son had the birthright. That meant that he would become the family leader when the father died and would receive twice as much inheritance as any other son.

DISCIPLE–A disciple is someone who accepts another person's teachings. In this way, a disciple "follows" the teacher. Those who accepted what Jesus taught were His disciples. The "twelve disciples" were not the only ones. Jesus had many disciples, but the twelve were special followers whom He chose to lead the others after He went back to heaven.

DOUBT–When we have faith, we are sure that what a person says is true. When we doubt, we are not sure.

FLAX–Flax is a plant. When the stalks are dried, the fibers in their "bark" are used to make linen cloth. In Bible times flax was usually laid upon a rooftop to dry.

LAMP–In Bible times there were no electric lights, wax candles, flashlights, or gas lamps. Lamps were small pottery or metal dishes. Some were open dishes; some were covered, with two holes in the top. In one hole, in the center, olive oil was poured. In the other hole, at the end, a wick was placed and lighted.

LOAVES–Loaves of bread in Jesus' time were small and flat, like thick pancakes.

MONUMENT–Any object that reminds us of someone or something special. Usually monuments are made of stone, but not always.

OIL–The kind of oil used in engines today was not used in Bible times. Oil for lamps was squeezed from olives. Sometimes perfume was added to give a pleasant scent.

PROMISED LAND–The land of Canaan, which God promised to the Israelites. After the Exodus, He led them there and helped them settle in the land until the time of the Exile.

SYNAGOGUE–The name of a building where Jewish people worship. Jesus and His neighbors worshiped in synagogues, as well as in the Temple in Jerusalem.

TALENT–Today we speak of a talent as the ability to do something. In Bible times a talent was a large sum of money, about seventy-five pounds of gold, more than a half million dollars. Gold was not always in coin form, but sometimes in the form of jewelry or broken chunks.